RICHARD PRICE:
NEW YORK A.M.

Midway through FREEDOMLAND—the second of Richard Price's
three novels set in the fictional New Jersey city Dempsey—an ambitious
local reporter scrutinizes the apartment of a mother grieving over
the disappearance of her young son. The journalist runs her hand
over 'tapes, posters, tabletops, dishes' for the 'tactile connection' they
provide to the woman she's studying. 'She thought of all reporters,'
the novel goes on to say, as people

> who were addicted to something she thought of as the Infilling—the
> compulsive hankering to witness, to absorb, to taste human behavior
> in extremis; the desire to embrace, to be filled with, no matter how
> fleetingly, the power of human grief; human rage; to experience it over
> and over; to absorb the madness of others, the commitment of others,
> the killers, the killed, the bereaved, the stunned, the liars, the fuckers,
> the heroes, the clownish, and the helpless. Jesse needed these people to
> come inside her, to give her life, *a* life, and she loved them for it.

'The compulsive hankering to witness' would be a good
description for the impulse that gives energy to Price's nine novels
and his numerous scripts for film and TV. Born in the Bronx in
1949, he studied at Cornell University and in the writing program
at Columbia University; by the time he graduated from the latter
in 1974, when he was 24, he had already published his first book of
fiction, THE WANDERERS, a portrait of young gang members in
a Bronx housing project much like the one in which he grew up.

There followed three fast-talking novels of New York—
BLOODBROTHERS (1976), LADIES' MAN (1978), and THE
BREAKS (1983)—each about a man for whom the city, as the
novelist Michael Chabon put it, 'demarcates the upper limit of what
he can imagine and the depth to which he can sink.' Burned-out after

this run of productivity and struggling with a debilitating cocaine habit, Price withdrew from novel writing, accepted an offer to compose the script for Martin Scorsese's pool hall drama THE COLOR OF MONEY in 1986, and took up a second career as a screenwriter.

It was during these years writing for the movies that Price developed something of a reporter's urge to take 'a life' from other people and examine the fault lines between them—'the killers, the killed, the bereaved.' The three Dempsey novels that followed— CLOCKERS (1992), FREEDOMLAND (1998), and SAMARITAN (2003)—emerged out of close engagement with people at work in Jersey City: cops; cocaine dealers; teachers; detectives; housing project residents struggling to go about their lives unharassed. Race became a dominant subject.

Each novel shuttles back and forth between two juxtaposed central figures, one white and one black: a homicide cop and a drug-corner lieutenant (CLOCKERS); the mother who's lost her son and the detective on the hunt for him (FREEDOMLAND); a daft, altruistic classroom volunteer and the female officer who takes up his case after he gets severely beaten (SAMARITAN).

Price has often been praised as a peerless writer of dialogue. His ear for the rhythms of human speech is on fine display in TV shows such as THE NIGHT OF—which he co-created with Steven Zaillian—and THE WIRE, which he started writing for after the show drew heavily on CLOCKERS for inspiration about the workings of the street-level drug trade. But the Dempsey novels and the two New York-set studies of crime and punishment that followed them, LUSH LIFE (2008) and THE WHITES (2015), confirmed that he was just as skilled a writer of place, locale, and décor. To read Price is to be immersed in the texture and trappings of successive layers of urban life—to absorb, from how people talk, dress, and make their homes, what they need and resent about the cities they inhabit.

He has always been a fastidious chronicler of specific New York neighborhoods as they transform under new influxes of capital and real estate. There are the seedy Times Square sex clubs where the hero of LADIES' MAN takes refuge, or the swiftly gentrifying, patchwork Lower East Side in LUSH LIFE where the paths of bartenders, dealers, and cops collide. His next novel is set in Harlem, where he shares a brownstone with his wife, the journalist and fiction writer Lorraine Adams. It was there that I met Price. Our conversation kept returning to the neighborhood, its future, and that of New York itself. Price's characters, too, rarely keep themselves from speaking their mind about where they live. 'I hate this fuckin' city,' one says about Dempsey in FREEDOMLAND. 'This city's got no heart.'

How is your Harlem novel coming together?

I've been writing it on and off for a few years and I'm through with the first draft. The problem is, as I get to know Harlem better, what was 'novel' to me ten years ago now seems like the hyped ruminations of a tourist. Normally, once I find a story I want to commit years of my life to writing, I go out of my way to embed myself 24/7 in the world of my characters—but I live in Harlem and have been since 2008, and at this point I don't know who's embedding who anymore. The more I absorb up here by just going about my life, the more the story shifts in focus, scale, and tone. All I know is this—I don't want it to be my so-called 'Harlem Novel'. It makes me feel like I'm some kind of half-assed Columbus 'discovering' the New World. And I don't want to chase LUSH LIFE with another panoramic doorstopper about a specific community. My knees couldn't take it.

Is it different writing about Harlem than, say, Jersey City or the Lower East Side?

Yeah. With Jersey City I could do whatever I wanted because I'd fictionalized it, so I wasn't beholden to actual people and places and things. I didn't want it be a *roman à clef*-slash-guessing game, like a down and out VALLEY OF THE DOLLS, with everyone trying to figure out which character is Judy Garland. The intent was to use a Jersey City-like model as a stand-in for the mid-sized American city nearest to the reader, since the urban dynamics of the place are pretty much the same coast to coast. Harlem isn't a stand-in like Dempsey, but except for the actual streets and ancient histories, the place is just a backdrop for straight-up fiction.

What kind of research have you been doing?

The research I do is the research I always do: I hang out. Every once in a while I want to talk to a particular individual, or to be present for a certain thing that's happening. But basically it's all about osmosis. I always

You lose that sense of wonder.

quote Jimmy Breslin in his biography of Damon Runyon: 'He did what all good reporters do. He hung out.'

In the late 1980s, when I wrote the screenplay for SEA OF LOVE, I did ride-alongs with cops and I started seeing more of the world than I ever thought I would. Your first reaction is that your jaw drops. But then you need to get to that point where your jaw isn't dropping anymore. In the beginning, everything you see is explosive. But you have to get past that until what you see becomes routine, and the nuances start to reveal themselves.

The sense of wonder never leaves me, but the truth of a place is in the small stuff, always the small stuff. So I'm out there with the neighbors, just hanging out, having conversations with people, seeing what pops for me.

Occasionally I'll go to something I hadn't planned on doing. It might be a church or a funeral service or a meeting open to the community. For example, I became friends with a guy, an ex-con, who runs a grassroots Stop the Violence organization. It puts together block rallies within a day or two on any street in Harlem or the Bronx where a shooting has gone down. He also has a contract with the city to conduct anti-violence workshops at the Bronx County probation office. I would go with him to both, again and again, until I had an understanding for the near hopelessness of his efforts. But I also gained an appreciation for the power of his optimism, in the face of the monumental personal despair and bureaucratic indifference he chose to confront. Talk about tilting at windmills. His relentless buoyancy was almost frightening.

For me, it's all about discovering and understanding things that I wasn't even looking for. But I recognize them when I see them, when I hear them. I need to be ever present. I love being out there more than anything else. At the end of the day I'm still writing fiction, but for me all the electricity is in the learning process.

Do you know when you come across something that will find its way into your fiction?

Yeah, but I don't even think about that. By now, I just gut-know that this thing is a lot more than what it may seem on the surface. It's all instinct.

I once went with a detective to see a psychic for a triple murder. It was hilarious, and slightly spooky, but what this psychic did was hold an object belonging to one of the victims. She would go into a rocking half-trance, and then burst into this obscene rant about the killer—'that cocksucker, that motherfucker…!' In the middle of this verbal cesspool barrage she'd blurt out a random noun, like 'Tires!' or 'Mailbox!' And that word was supposed to be a key clue from the beyond. After which she'd say, 'I have no idea why I said that, but it's a piece of the puzzle. You're the detective, it's your job to put all the pieces together.'

It's the same thing: If somebody says something to you, they might say it, but that's the end of their thought. They might not know the resonance of what they just said, but for you it's a gobsmacker. My job is to take that and use it to enhance a section of my puzzle.

When you put these puzzle pieces together, do you find genre conventions useful? Your books often resemble crime novels, but none of them seem to quite fit that description. They are just as much New York novels.

One strategic problem in writing about a place is how to avoid getting lost in its enormity. How can I embrace panorama without becoming panoramic? I don't consider myself a crime writer per se, but a crime is often structurally a blessing, because a police investigation is both chronological and orderly. It pulls in people from everywhere: witnesses, victims, perps, cops, business owners, pedestrians, people hanging out of windows. A proper criminal investigation can be an excellent horse to ride through a chaotic landscape.

Having said that, I've never really been interested in plot. It's almost an afterthought. I was working on CLOCKERS for a year and a half, not writing yet, but building it, and I had no idea what the story was. I just knew *where* I was, was the right place. But these days I prefer to have my story, at least loosely, figured out in advance. That doesn't mean that things won't start switching up on me the minute I put pen to paper, but I like to delude myself into thinking that I have this thing down cold.

How do you go about giving the story a structure?

I found in CLOCKERS and FREEDOM-LAND that if you have a big, dense landscape, splitting points of view between two oppositional characters will give the story a kind of perpetual velocity. Here's one character: This is where they're coming from, and this is their investment in the unfolding tale. Then you bring in the second character and provide their agenda *vis-à-vis* the tale, and here is their personal baggage. And this second individual has knowledge that the first individual has no access to. From here, you seesaw the points of view between these two players, overlapping at times but always advancing the storyline as the events unfold. It's akin to building a Jenga tower.

And you fill out the structure using what you observed on the street?

Yeah, kind of. But when I go out there I don't have any questions. I don't have a program or a to-do list. With CLOCKERS, I kinda sorta had a list, I very much wanted to know how this and that worked. But even then, what I wrote about was the stuff I wasn't planning on. Because I don't know yet what I don't know, if that makes sense. At first you go out there like a blank slate.

Are these moments ever too loaded? Would they ever seem too implausible transposed into a novel?

But after a time I can at least begin to identify the arenas of my ignorance and begin focusing on the right questions. Every day out there for me is like jumping into a mosh pit. Every day out there is loaded.

Well, it depends whether you believe God is a first-rate novelist or a second-rate novelist. Just because something happens doesn't make it art. I remember back in the '90s, I had a friend who was an emergency medical technician coming out of Metropolitan Hospital on 99th Street, and he let me come for a ride-along in his ambulance. This was at the height of the crack era, and he had a run regarding a woman having a seizure on the corner of 117th Street and Third Avenue. So we go. And sure enough, there was a woman convulsing on the sidewalk, and it was horrible. She was flat on her back helplessly spasming and foaming at the mouth, and all these people were standing around, including kids, just laughing at her. So they get the woman inside the bus, take her vitals, and shoot her back to the hospital. And the supervisor starts yelling at my friend, 'Where the fuck is the woman?'

My guy says back, 'What are you talking about? She's right here!'

'Oh yeah? Where'd you pick her up?'

'118th and Third.'

'No kidding,' the supervisor says. 'I said *117th* and Third.'

It turns out, there was another woman one block south having the same seizure.

As a writer of fiction, what do you do with something like that? It sounds contrived, it sounds bogus. As I said, just because it happened doesn't make it art.

THE BRONX

Let's rewind to your earlier books.
You published your first novel,
THE WANDERERS, at 24.

When I was younger, my novels and how they were received were all too important to my sense of self. But over the years, as I became more anchored and secure and committed to other facets of existence, they've taken their proper place on the pie chart of self-worth. In the last twenty years, with raising children and finding—pardon the expression—true love, I have gained a somewhat more relaxed attitude about their reception. I love to write, that'll never change, but I have a fuller life. Earlier, there was something missing for me that my novels and their acclaim were compensating for. It was unhealthy.

Do you think that had anything to do with the fact that the books you wrote in the 1970s were much more autobiographical?

Yeah. All I knew about was me—and I didn't know me very well. That's why I stopped writing those books. I was tapped out. After four novels in nine years, with my life as my only reference point, what else could I possibly write about? What I had for breakfast? I felt like I had to stop. My tongue was hanging out.
What I wrote at 24 had a lot of energy and a lot of pizzazz, but when I look back on my books from the '70s I flinch. All I can see is: How did I get away with that? But then, I was 24. I had a 24 year-old brain. You're probably not 24 yet.

Hey…

No, I'm just saying, I'm doing the math.

I am, in fact, 24.

Well, no offense, but what does a 24 year-old know about anything?

Shit.

When I taught creative writing—by the way, Thomas McGuane once said, 'I've done a lot of terrible things in my life but I never taught creative writing…' Anyway, when I taught creative writing, I quickly came to realize that all I could do that was in any way helpful was to question why a student chose to write about a particular thing, when perhaps what they really wanted to write about was something else. So, you try to help them find the true story that was driving their desire to become a writer in the first place—very young writers tend to flail about before they come close to anything resembling their voice and subject. Even if I succeeded on that front—which wasn't often—there was the impossible task of injecting them with life experience serum. You can't teach somebody to be twenty years older than they are. I mean, you have to live some more, swallow some more of the world. That doesn't mean you can't be some kind of *enfant terrible*, but, using myself as an example: If only someone could have injected me with experience beyond my years, perhaps I wouldn't have to read my earlier books through a peephole.

THE BREAKS was your last novel before you withdrew from books for some time.

That, for me, was the most egregious. If I squint, I can see what I did well, but what I did poorly is as big as an elephant. With THE BREAKS, I was trying too hard to just have another book out. It's like, what are you trying to say with this book? I was trying to say, 'I really want to be published.' It was too panicky, too showy, had too much shtick. On top of which I was struggling with cocaine addiction at that time, which was like wearing a gasoline jacket to a bonfire.

That's when you went to Hollywood?

Well, I've never been in LA for more than 72 continuous hours in my life. But yeah, I had a lot of offers to write scripts, so I started taking on jobs. People had been asking me to write screenplays since 1974, when THE WANDERERS came out—basically because my dialogue was so 'authentic'. It's nice to have a gift for dialogue if you're a screenwriter, but it's not that important. Actors will give you good dialogue. Even if you write, say, okay dialogue—if an actor is good, he or she will make it sound much better than it deserves. Good lines add zip on paper, but the key job of a screenplay is to provide a shapely narrative structure. It's all about structure and momentum. Somebody once described a script to me as a pyramid. You have, say, three or four people at the base, and they all have to meet at the top in two hours. Some fall off the mountain, some get to plant a flag. That's more important than good dialogue writing.

That's the thing. There's a tremendous difference between human speech and written dialogue. Good written dialogue is not about authentic speech—a tape recorder will give you that, and it'll most likely sound both boring and near incomprehensible. Good written dialogue cheats authentic speech, nudges it into a certain shapeliness without sacrificing its flow. The eye hears. However, we're talking about dialogue on the page. If you take that wonderful speech on page 24 and put it in an actor's mouth, it'll most likely sound wooden, as in, written.

You can read great dialogue in a novel and the words just fly off the page, but when those same deathless sentences come out of an actor's mouth they can sound overcooked. They can sound prosaic and artificial. However terse you think your written exchanges are, they're invariably too wordy for performance. One of my most embarrassing learning experiences was in the early '90s, hearing the actors at a read-through rehearsal for the film MAD DOG AND GLORY. At first, when they were just *reading* my script, everybody loved their lines—but the minute they

> I imagine there's an important difference between writing for the page and writing for a human voice.

started to *speak* their lines, the writtenness was so obvious that half the dialogue just dropped like lead on the table. At one point Robert De Niro was reading a monologue for his character. He got about halfway through and said, 'Wait, hold on… I'm *still talking* now?' It's a humbling experience to hear your written dialogue in an actor's mouth, but an important lesson—never write three words when one will do.

How does writing a screenplay compare to writing a novel?

There is no writing in a screenplay. You don't write a screenplay. There's no prose in a screenplay, no narrative, no internal dialogue. Basically it's 120 pages of Post-it notes for the director and the actors. It's two-dimensional. A book is four-dimensional. It takes you into the interior of the character's thoughts, and has a narrative voice that can offer exposition. But a movie is two-dimensional. People say things and do things. End of story.

Is it easier or more comfortable writing for TV series, at least, because you have so much more of a scope over which to develop the characters?

The biggest and most inaccurate comment *du jour* is that episodic TV is the new novel. TV is the screen; TV is two-dimensional. It's only like a novel in the sense that the weekly installments are structured as progressive chapters. That's it.

However, I'm grateful for that eight to ten hour length, because the thing I hate about screenplay writing, especially if I'm adapting my own stuff—which I should never do, I only did it because I couldn't turn down the money—is that it is torture to reduce a book of 400 pages, dense with event and interiority, to two hours of Post-it notes. I can adapt somebody else's book because I have no personal stake in the material. I read the Walter Tevis novel THE COLOR OF MONEY once, put it down, and never looked at it again. But adapting my own stuff will take me as long as writing the first draft of a new book, where any other reasonably experienced screenwriter adapting a novel of mine could probably bang it out in a few months.

By the way, HBO is hoping to doing LUSH LIFE as a miniseries.

Really?

Um hm.

Who else is involved with it?

Me.

Very good.

It's supposed to be an eight-parter like THE DEUCE. Eight hours, 60 pages per episode, is 460 pages. But it's 460 pages of 'Say this, do that.' It's not like I'm writing a 460-page book by any stretch.

How are you conceiving of this one visually? Are there any specific color palettes or styles or tones that you have in mind when you work on a series?

Right now all I'm thinking about is writing. Over the years I had a few chances to direct, or be a proactive producer, AKA set-rat, but I'm a writer, you know. And a writer writes. So when you ask about palette and style, that's down the line, and done by people who actually know what they're doing.

Do you interact with them, though?

Mainly in the beginning, and just with the director and actors, when everyone's still trying to grasp the right approach. After that…

Because it affects so much how the writing is perceived. For instance, the visual mood of THE NIGHT OF is much gloomier than how I think of most of your novels.

Well, listen, that's thanks to Steven Zaillian, who co-created and directed THE NIGHT OF. As great as it was, all I can to take credit for is the script. But TV is for the eye—you're watching, not reading the story. You hand in the screenplay, and if you are not otherwise actively and aggressively involved in its dramatic transformation— which is a choice—then you're at the mercy of whoever is in charge. Zaillian just happened to be really good.

P
ZEST
ZEST
LeSabre

PLEASANT VER
11

PLEASANT AV

NY
I ♥ PUERTO

Joseph Rodriguez: El Barrio

Born and raised in Brooklyn, Joseph
Rodriguez is an internationally renowned
photographer whose work on global and
American subcultures spans the past four
decades. In his twenties he worked as
a cab driver in New York, documenting all
that he saw with his camera. The resulting
images—telling stories of afterhours clubs,
families, gangs, and street artists—are
synonymous with 1980s New York. The
series SPANISH HARLEM illustrates
the latter half of the decade in the Latino
district El Barrio. It is the product of
spending long periods of time with his
subjects, often without a camera, conveying
a sense of openness and intimacy.

It's got to be frustrating from a writer's point of view if a film doesn't turn out the way you intended it to.

The thing about film is that it goes through the hands of so many people before it's finished. The casting. The directing, the cinematography. The editing room. I mean, if you have a two-hour movie, you're making that from 200 hours of film. So if you give the same 200 hours of film to ten different film editors and directors, you're gonna get ten different movies.

The first couple of times you feel ripped off by the end product you're allowed to be outraged. But after that you know the score, and you have no right to sing, 'Look what they did to my song, Ma.' After getting burned a few times you have the choice: You can quit the business altogether; you can be realistic about things, but decide that the money trumps the hair-pulling; or you can keep buying lottery tickets, praying for the stars to align and give you a big critical winner, glory on high. At the end of the day, so much is out of your hands that writing a script is akin to buying a lottery ticket.

A lot of screenwriters become directors, because aspiring to be a screenwriter is like aspiring to be vice president. You're the low man on the totem pole. If that's all you do, very often you'll feel like, 'I have to go up the food chain or I'm gonna kill myself.' On the other hand, no one individual ever has complete control. The screenwriter is at the mercy of the actors and directors, the directors are at the mercy of the studio, the studio is at the mercy of their investors, and everybody is at the mercy of the ticket buyers.

But I always feel like I'm a novelist first and foremost, so my sense of self is never at stake. In general, when it comes to doing TV and film, I'm good to go.

JERSEY CITY

In 1992 you published your first book in nine years, CLOCKERS. What made you want to return to writing novels after such a long time?

After years of surrendering my scripts to the higher powers out there, of constantly steeling myself for the inevitable changes to my work in order to accommodate various commercial and practical realities, I had finally found a story—CLOCKERS—that I was afraid to turn over to the too many cooks in the studio kitchen. I had something that required absolute control, absolute ownership. I needed to say goodbye to Hollywood—kinda, sorta—and sit down for a few years and write another novel.

CLOCKERS was the first of a loose trilogy, the Dempsey books. And a turning point, in that you changed your source material from there on. Did that require an accompanying change in the approach to the prose itself?

I'd been away from novels for eight years since THE BREAKS, had success as a screenwriter, and, obviously, stopped doing coke. The old saw that I had lived by—'Write what you know'—had boxed me into a corner. But in those eight years between THE BREAKS and CLOCKERS, what I had personally experienced—marriage, raising two daughters, beating drug addiction, becoming financially secure via my success in films, just *experiencing* steady success—quintupled 'what I know.' And then it came to me: Just go out in the world, expose yourself to whatever interests you and *voilà*, that becomes 'what you know' too. I also decided to liberate myself from the burden of self-reference by leaving myself out of things altogether. Step off the field and become a literary reporter.

The next milestone was finding a literary voice, a prose style that would provide a counterpoint to the heaviness of all that reported observation. That's when Hubert Selby Jr.'s LAST EXIT TO BROOKLYN came into my life like a beacon. Here's this guy, an individual who stumbled into the writing life in the 1950s, a working class ex-merchant marine who found himself writing about 'what he knew'—a down and out, urban redneck slice of hell. A subject that would normally lend itself to social realism, especially back then. But Selby was also a jazzhead, and so he adopted an incantatory narrative voice suffused with a bebop lyricism, lifting that dense, brooding tale reeking of social reportage into a sax riff of a book. That to me was the way to go; to counteract the density of my own story of urban woe with a narrative style that lifted and zoomed. The trick, of course, being that the style should never overwhelm the substance.

It's interesting that the three Dempsey books all have this recurring character who's an interloper—the actor in CLOCKERS, the journalist in FREEDOMLAND, the writer in SAMARITAN. Why did each of those books seem to need this character who's outside of the world they address?

Well, it's sort of like WHERE'S WALDO. Where's the author. You look at all the characters: hey, there he is, a little bit of Kilroy Was Here, or Alfred Hitchcock coming off a bus. It's a little bit of self-parody. But a little bit goes a long way. I always found myself in trouble when I made myself the centerpiece of anything. In SAMARITAN, I totally fell back into that trap. I was attempting to write a book based on a personal dilemma, with characters as stand-ins playing out my own issues. I look at that book now and I'd chop out a third.

It was too autobiographical?

I was deeply drawn to the characters and the dilemmas contained in SAMARITAN. If I wasn't, how could I have written it? But yeah, there was too much of me. Better to stay clear, to let the characters run the show.

However, I loved that grounding in what I saw around me, and what I could do with what I saw. I always loved social realism. When I was a teenager, I loved all these protest novels about life in the city. I was from the city, but I had a hard time finding the city in my public school reading lists. I couldn't find anything in those boilerplate reading assignments that offered a confirmation of what I knew. I believe some of us read in order to find ourselves, our experiences, mirrored in the lives of others. That recognition provides a great validation that not only are we human, but that we have existed for centuries before ourselves. That we are not freaks, we are not isolated, and that we belong. Think of adolescents back in the day—how they seized on a gloomy, reflective, and alienated character like Holden Caulfield in THE CATCHER IN THE RYE. The life-saving, self-identifying recognition offered by that prep-school drop out. But Holden never did it for me, the way that LAST EXIT TO BROOKLYN did. Hubert Selby Jr. was not a writer born, but he nailed his characters to the floor. Eye, ear, gesture, musicality, the core of their core. And he wrote about a world that I knew. As a result, after reading LAST EXIT TO BROOKLYN I realized that most social realism was too earnest by half, and too humorless. There was no jazz in that genre. Reading those books felt like sawing wood. The whole point of them was to make a point. It was like Soviet poster art but without the colors. Selby offered me a way to shed all that wet cement.

So anyway, starting with the Dempsey novels, I had to stop writing like a kid. The books, without sacrificing any zip, had to be more serious, more focused. I say the books had to be more sober, but at the same time they had to be sharp and have their own kind of realism and bebop.

The realism seems to go hand in hand with this documentary streak running through all of your novels: I was rereading a chapter in THE WHITES in which an apartment is being very closely inspected and its contents laid out. And then I remembered how many of your books all have scenes in which apartments get anatomized. It's almost a reporter's approach.

I first did that in 1974, in THE WANDERERS, where I was itemizing everything on the dinner table. I like inventory because it's not just the objects; you're not just making a list. The assemblage says something about the culture and the character of those who are sitting around that table. It reveals their sense of place in the world.

But it's also about the environment and the setting and the period. The books written in the '90s are very suggestive about the décor of that time.

In a way they become time capsules. Just the disarray of a bathroom tells you something, or how things were arranged in the living room. I never just throw a detail in there for the sake of throwing it in there. I'm not an out of control camera. But if I think something is telling, I'll tell it.

And that's a reporting impulse, too: to survey a scene and look at the details that seem suggestive.

Well, half the time it's because I've been in a hundred different apartments like that. The other half of the time it's because I have an imagination. You know, it is called fiction.

HARLEM

I read somewhere that you would never do a historical novel.

I'm too obsessive about getting things right. I can't write about something I don't know intimately, so historical novels are beyond me.

But do you do some historical research for the books, to get a sense of the neighborhoods and their past?

I kind of just know that stuff. To write about the Lower East Side, I don't say: maybe I should read Jacob Riis, or Lincoln Steffens, or the social reformers, or CALL IT SLEEP, or THE RISE OF DAVID LEVINSKY. No. It's just stuff I've absorbed. Sometimes someone tells me something in conversation, and if it's interesting I'll look it up in a little more detail, but that's as far as it goes.

What's your view on Harlem during the past ten years you have been living here? As with the Lower East Side, you are writing about Harlem at a time when it is undergoing a rapid transformation.

Michael Greenberg in the NEW YORK REVIEW did interviews with a lot of tenants in Crown Heights, Brownsville, and East New York as the developers have been pouring in. And one woman who was getting forced out of her apartment on Schenectady Avenue told him, 'We watched over this street, we cleaned it up. Why should we have to leave?'

One of the detectives in the 32, the Harlem precinct, told me that the two greatest crime-fighters in this city are sheetrock and cranes. You have people living in Harlem all their lives, multi-generational, and all this new construction, all these new businesses —it's not for them. Every time they see trees being planted, it's not for them. It's for the people who are coming. And they'll be white, for the most part.

In what city can you not give voice to that sentiment? There are homeowners who moved to Harlem at the worst of times, a black couple, say: their children are grown, they're in retirement, and they live in a brownstone, yes—but they were here in the crack days. They were here in the heroin '70s. They were here through all of it and they held fast. And now they're older, their children are gone, and they have less income. They might have bought that turn of the century brownstone for $30,000 in 1968 but now they can't afford any more infrastructure repairs, so it's probably in bad shape. Then someone knocks on your door and offers you a million bucks.

The buyers are mainly interested in the land rights so they'll probably tear that place down—but how could you say no? The thing is, are they going to live in New York? Nope. They're going to go back down south, because whatever they pay you to buy your place, that's how much you have to get another. So everybody's going back to Carolina. Virginia. Maryland. Harlem was enough of a moonscape during the very bad years, but these people kept it from being a complete moonscape. These are the people who kept churches in business and went to work every day. They were the stabilizers in a troubled, chaotic time. But real estate wants what it wants and that's that.

Nobody I know who was living on the Lower East Side in 2005 could afford to live in it now. It was still a microclimate then. Starting in the 1970s, you had young people coming into a funky neighborhood because they're young and want adventure in their life. They want to feel like they're having an experience. They're creative. And they enjoy the frisson of living in a down at the heels community. To walk down Orchard Street or Ludlow Street in 2003 or 2004 was really different; it was exciting because of the mix and match. Then when real estate people come in, they smell the espresso and it all goes to hell.

LUSH LIFE was very much about that, these two different worlds colliding in the Lower East Side.

Well, I was there. The book took place in 2005. The Lower East Side was just starting to get these flashy hotels, and more and more young people coming in—those who used to be called white pioneers. But the whole notion of these arrivistes coming face to face with projects people, with people on economic life support and visa versa, each group cocooned in their own cultural *shetl*—that collision of realities was where the drama lived for me at that time. But that was then. Now, it's about business, it's about real estate, and it's over. It's like being in Soho in the '70s. Fresh and raw and rife with possibility, but now it looks like a playground for New Jersey dentists coming in on the weekend with their families, everybody walking around scarfing down waffle cones and window-shopping all the high-end chain stores.

But you don't think Harlem is going to follow exactly the same path.

I always feel that Harlem is too vast. It goes from river to river. It's not the Lower East Side, which is 0.7 miles. It's too vast and too historical, too much of a spiritual and cultural mecca in the imagination. But I dunno. Nothing is being built for the people who have always lived here. None of these condos, none of these restaurants. Sheetrock and cranes. Real estate wants what it wants, it's like trying to hold back water with your hands.

LOWER EAST SIDE

Your characters don't go off about politics very often.

Well, because I'm not writing an editorial. I never want to write as if I'm telling people what to think about what I write. What I feel is, you write about the thing, and let people decide what they think about it. I prefer the politics to come through the actions of the characters.

The politics are embedded in the story and setting.

How do you write a novel about a city and not have a novel about race? What's true in one city is true in all cities. It's human beings in an urban environment. It's about race; it's about class; it's about law and order; it's about politics. What happens here is the exact same dynamic, just maybe with a different geography or visuality. Baltimore has alleys; New York doesn't have alleys. The cops' hats in Chicago sport a checkerboard pattern; cops in Texas, Louisiana, sport mirror shades and Stetsons. It's all the same.

The other night I went to a performance of James Joyce's THE DEAD at the American Irish Historical Society. There was a quote from Joyce in the program: 'For myself, I always write about Dublin, because if I can get to the heart of Dublin

I can get to the heart of all the cities of the world. In the particular is contained the universal.' I read it and thought, 'This is how I've been operating since 1974.' It's the particular. You trust in the particular to say so much more than its particular self. And you take a city like New York, or a neighborhood like the Lower East Side, or you make up your own city. I always felt like the city had to stand in for every city. It's no good to write about Jersey City or Dempsey unless someone 3,000 miles away reads it and thinks of Oakland.

But you only get there by asserting the particular aspects of that city.

Yeah. Every particular aspect is gonna find its cousin. Like—this is something I experienced when I was writing LUSH LIFE. I was going home with these two undercover cops after they checked out. We were going to go to a bar, and they were riding up Ludlow Street, or one of the north-south streets on the Lower East Side. And they see a black guy on a bicycle with a white kid sitting on the handlebars. It was about midnight. The cops look at each other, pull the guy over, and say, 'What's the story?'

The black guy was a bartender at one of the Keith McNally restaurants, and the kid was, like, a second- or third-generation hippie kid. The cops separated the two, and they were brutal with the guy. It was so humiliating. They were trying to intimidate the shit out of him. They had the kid separate, and I kept going back and forth between them. The kid didn't understand what was going on; but he was talking. And when he started saying, 'Sometimes I'm alone with him,' the cop suddenly wondered if this child was being molested. He starts pushing the kid: 'What else do you do together? You can tell me.' He shows his badge, 'Do you know what this is? I'm a policeman. Nothing bad's gonna happen.'

The kid was a nervous wreck, and when he sees the badge he bursts into tears.

And the cops are like, 'We've got him.' But the kid says, 'If you motherfuckers harass my mom's boyfriend one more time, just because he's black and I'm not...' It turned out that the kid's mother was this guy's girlfriend. He just about lived with them. There was nothing wrong; he was just picking up this kid from a sleepover date after his shift was finished.

And the kid just tore the cops a new asshole. He's screaming at them, 'He took me to a street fair and the police thought he kidnapped me. The cops pulled him out of my apartment because the lady next door said a black man was raping my mom.' And the cops are, like, freaking out. But every time the black guy calls out, 'You okay there, buddy?' the cop standing over him says, 'Hey, what did I tell you about talking to him?' Finally, they called the mother, and *she* starts freaking out: It's 12:30 in the morning, her kid isn't home. 'Oh my god, what happened?' And the cop says, 'Oh, no, no, no, we're just checking, you know, he was—neither of them had bicycle helmets on, and it's a safety violation.' The mother almost had a nervous breakdown. Eventually they let the guy and the kid go. I got back in the car with them, and they're riding in silence for about three more blocks, and then one cop looks to the other and says, 'You know what? I *still* think there's something fishy about those two.'

So why do I have to write about politics? How much does that tell you about so many things? That's my idea of writing about politics.

It's striking how nuanced your depictions of these situations are, particularly when you write about cops. There's such careful attention to the practical details of their line of work, and how it wears them out.

Most of the cops I hung out with when I was writing CLOCKERS are retired. I mean, they still could be middle-aged, but after twenty years you're done, and you get half of your salary for life. And if you go out on a medical you get three-quarters. If you broke your ankle in a chase, or if you hurt your back, or if you got shot, all of a sudden you get three-quarters of your highest salary for the rest of your life.

SEA OF LOVE is about that. Al Pacino's character is like, 'I'm a cop. I'm only 45 and I can cash out. What am I gonna do with the rest of my adult life?' It's like the ant and the grasshopper. Some cops won't think about it, and all of a sudden they're 45 and they have no plans. Some cops will say, 'I'm going to law school.' 'I'm studying for my real estate license.' 'I bought a bar.' These are the individuals who made plans for the next 20 years. The rest are like, 'I don't know what to do. I was a cop. Now I'm not. What beats being a cop? I'm lost.'

And some of them—like Pacino's character in that movie—get hooked on the job.

Well, that's the other thing. Being a cop is like being a rabbi or priest, or a doctor. It's a very glamorous thing to be. If you're at a cocktail party, and you're talking to people in the room and they ask what you do and you say, 'I'm a detective'—all of a sudden their brains go: *detective*. 'I'm a rabbi.' 'I'm a surgeon.' These are jobs that freeze people's minds, because they make them think about all sorts of things. To be a cop is to be a star.

On the other side of the line, novels like CLOCKERS or FREEDOMLAND give a very differentiated and complex view of the projects.

CLOCKERS, FREEDOMLAND, and SAMARITAN are all about prevailing counterpoints on either side of a color line. It's a matter of how much Other is the Other. Race relations have been an obsession of mine since childhood. When I was a kid my parents were very conservative and they filled me with a lot of paranoia. I grew up in a housing project; we all went up the same elevators, went to the same schools, ate the same food for dinner, played ball together. But even in a housing project there was the Other, and the kids started to socially separate by race pretty early on. I got the feeling that very few parents encouraged racial harmony on either side of the color line. And each race had its own notion of what it meant to 'protect' their children.

As a white writer writing about race you have to acknowledge where you're coming from, which is a white life perspective. You have to have a healthy respect for what you have never experienced and never will. But that doesn't mean you can't create characters simply because they're not your race or gender or your religious persuasion. A writer's mandate is to imagine lives not their own. It's called using your imagination. It's called empathy. It's called knowing your neighbor. It's called hanging out. And that's what I'm about.

It's reporting the novel.

One of the most difficult things to do when you're reporting a novel is to get your ass off the street and write. I so much prefer running with the wolves to a lot of my everyday not-hanging-out life. It's addictive. You feel that, if I stop here, tomorrow something's gonna happen that'll just zigzag clickety-clack through your head. And it's just: Stop. Stop. Just stop. Write. You know your shit backwards and forwards. What's the first sentence of your book?